C'mon
EVERYBODY
let's PLAY!

A GUIDE FOR FAMILY FUN,
FILLED WITH ACTIVITIES

Lizbeth Wright Albertson

Copyright © 2009 Lizbeth Wright Albertson
All rights reserved.

ISBN: 1-4392-5662-4
ISBN-13: 9781439256626

Visit www.booksurge.com to order additional copies.

Dedication

This book is dedicated:

To my mother, Connie Wright, who taught me the true meaning of fun.

To my three wonderful sons, Jake, Tyler, and Tucker, who bring joy to my life.

To my husband, Joe, who supported my challenge of writing this book.

To all the children and families who deserve to have play in their lives.

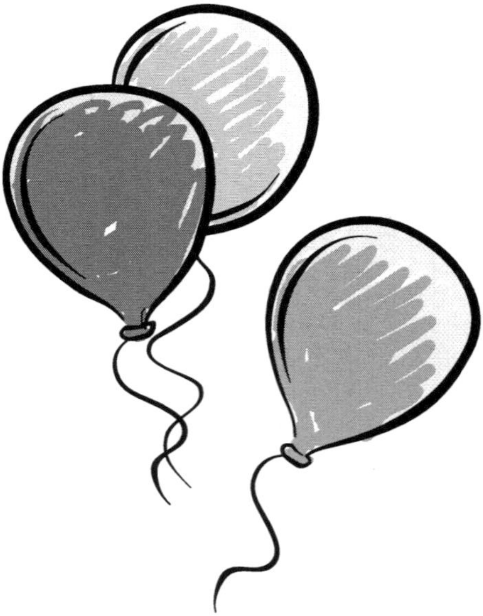

Acknowledgements

I would like to thank my dear friends, Amy, Sue and Lynn, for their encouragement and support.

Also I would like to say thank you to Gretchen Goodman who gave me the "push" I needed to write this book.

Contents

Dedication	iii
Acknowledgments	v
Introduction	ix
The Importance of Play	1
Working Parents/Busy Families	5
Children at Work	11
Developing Social Skills	19
Disciplined Play	23
Outdoor Play and Organized Sports	27
Teen Play	33
Homework vs. Play	39
Technology and Media	45
Play in the Adult World	49
Including All Children	53
Conclusion	57
Activities	59

Introduction

I have been an educator for over twenty years. I have seen many changes in our children, some good, some not so good. Many of these changes are brought about from societal issues. As a parent and educator, to me the single most important thing, which is near and dear to my heart and lays the foundation for all learning, seems to be losing its place in our lives and our schools.

It is *play*. Yes, play, otherwise known as "a child's work." The simplest yet most complex teaching tool is slowly being squeezed out of many of our lives and our children's lives because of the changes in our world. I am worried and sad for them.

I want to re-introduce families, one and all, to the importance and joy of play.

No matter what ages you and your family are, please take this opportunity to make your lives more fun and fulfilling. Play is a crucial part of every stage of development from infant, to toddler, preschooler, school age, pre-teen, teen, young adult, adult, and senior citizen. Basically, you are never too young or too old to play.

So together let's bring some fun back into our lives. Not only will you enjoy it, but it will make you a better person and benefit your family more than you could ever imagine.

The Importance of Play

As a teacher and advocate of young children, I am a huge proponent of play. Throughout my years in education, I have constantly expressed how beneficial play is to children and the positive impact it has on their lives as they grow into adults. People, even other educators, underestimate the power of play. I have often heard some teachers at the secondary level make the comment that all we do in kindergarten is play. I wish they only knew how profound that statement truly is. If it were not for play, we, as individuals, certainly would not be where we are today.

Through play, children experience their world. When we face a new challenge, we want to practice it so we can become better at it and gain a better understanding. When children are young, we often forget that many things they do are new experiences, so making the experience into play helps to make it fun and meaningful at the same time. Children will re-enact experiences that they have seen or had through play. Watch them, you may even find them playing out something they saw you doing! Children can also create their own experiences through imaginative play. This is the time when children can be anyone (Spider-Man, Cinderella) or can do anything they desire (climb an ice cream mountain, have the biggest birthday party in the whole world). Developing one's imagination sets the gears in motion for cognitive and emotional development. Many of our wonderful inventions have come from great imaginations.

Play strengthens us in many ways. For example, play promotes development of the small and large muscles through physical activity, enhances cognitive or learning abilities, and promotes social and language development.

It seems obvious to many how playing with sidewalk chalk can make the fingers stronger, how jumping rope can enhance our legs and visual perception, and how puzzles help to learn math concepts. But far too often, the social part of play is forgotten. It is a huge component of play that happens more naturally. Play helps to develop our abilities for social interactions. Unfortunately, children are lacking socially more now than in the past. Many children are having a harder time sharing, taking turns, developing friendships, and being empathetic because they are not getting the opportunities to fine tune these extremely important life skills.

THE IMPORTANCE OF PLAY

Think for a minute about all the places you go in a day or all the people with whom you interact. Much of our time is spent in some kind of social situation. We have learned somewhere along the way how to act appropriately, most likely through play.

As young children, we were provided with the experiences and opportunities to play. Most of us had time to play in preschool, kindergarten, or even play groups that our parents provided for us. Unfortunately, times are different now and the opportunities for play have dwindled dramatically. Preschools and kindergartens are being required to prepare children for more rigorous academics than in the past. I am not disputing the importance of academics, but we cannot and must not forget the value of play and its place in educating the whole child in all areas of their development as functioning human beings.

It is great for a child to be well educated, but they also need verbal, social and life skills to survive independently in our world. One of the best ways for children of any age to develop these skills is through play. We can all attest to the fact that work is more enjoyable when it is fun. Play that is encouraged by adults can provide the verbal and social modeling that will enhance the learning process. This does not mean that you do the play for them—instead, let them experience it firsthand. A perfect example is letting children create a tea party using real or pretend props and reenacting their perceptions; this is a great opportunity for social awareness and using the language to support the situation. I have been privy to many conversations and interactions in my "play house" area, and within the last few years I have heard and seen things that were well beyond the years of kindergarteners. Remember as you play with your child to keep your language and activities age appropriate and most importantly don't forget about the wonderment of imagination.

When creating play opportunities for your family, remember there are many different situations in which you can engage. You can provide age group (peer play) with your children and some friends, family time where you as a family play together, a time for parent and child, and free play where play happens naturally. The opportunities are limitless. The more experiences you create for your children, the more knowledgeable and well rounded they will become.

Working Parents/Busy Families

Most families consist of a single parent who works or two working parents, which certainly makes life more hurried. When are we ever supposed to find any extra time or energy to play with our children? It usually falls last on our to-do list. I am sure many of you are thinking play is a luxury that you cannot afford time-wise or monetarily. I know exactly how you feel, as I am a working mom and I often count on my "second wind" to reenergize me. It is also important for children to learn that we don't have to buy "things" to have fun. I know that it's tough to convince children that they don't need to have the latest and greatest toy out there. We need to show them how to have fun with what we have.

We need to look at the bigger picture. How will the time I spend playing with my children benefit them and me? Although our intentions are good, this time goes all too fast, so take advantage of it while you can. Keep in mind that the laundry can wait and the dirty dishes aren't going anywhere, but those precious moments with our children can't wait—they will soon be gone forever.

As parents we have to be careful not to let job stress or financial woes pour onto our children. We need to maintain the innocence of their childhood. Many of us also feel the guilt of having to leave our children at day care. Taking the time to play with your family will certainly ease your anxieties as you experience the joy of being with them. I promise that when you participate with your children for fun and enjoyment, you will become lost in their wonderful world of play and imagination.

If play will enhance all of our lives, make us better human beings, and it's fun and usually free, how can we not then afford to spare a few minutes a day?

Children love to play. We love to play. Make experiences that will work for you and your family. Let the children play with pots and pans while you are cooking, play games in the car, find foods according to color at the grocery store. There are opportunities around us all the time; use them to your advantage.

I often see parents feeling the need to engage their children in many activities outside of school, which adds to our busy schedules. It's great for your child to pick an activity of interest and partake, but don't overdo it. Children get overloaded just as we do. We all need down time, whether it's relaxing while reading a book, day dreaming, or playing with dolls. Ask yourself, "Is this an activity that my child wants to do or do I want them to do it, and what is the purpose?" Hopefully the answers will sound like this: it's an interest of the child, and he/she enjoys it!

Play can be incorporated into your lives in a variety of ways. Play can be a spontaneous act, it can be done in small doses, or you can actually plan a play day or event. Make it a priority each day to give time to your family. Whatever way you chose, just do something. I promise you will not regret it for you or your children. I see the impact daily that play has on a child, and it is truly the easiest and most fun way to learn and grow.

I have provided some ideas for you to help in making the hectic times fun. These are just some basics, as there is an abundance of resources you can research. Parents typically have the hardest time distracting their children from unpleasant situations that they encounter daily. I chose to address those to make your outings more pleasant.

While riding in the car:
Each person counts to their age or their age plus ten or times ten (make it age appropriate). Clap the syllables in everyone's name.

C'MON EVERYBODY LET'S PLAY!

Sing songs but change the beginnings of each word to the same letter to make it silly (example: row, row row rour roat rently rown re ream...).

While waiting in line:
Find three people wearing blue, red, and then yellow.
Copy cat: the leader makes a series of body part tappings, then everyone has to try to remember it and copy it (tap head, knee, shoulder, toe). Each person gets a turn to be leader and change the parts tapped.

While sitting at a restaurant:
Let children write the food orders for fun on your paper.
Play "I spy" using the decorations in the restaurant.

While sitting in the doctor/dentist office:
Create a story (example: one person starts the story, and each person playing adds to it until it's finished).
Draw letters on each other's hand using your finger, then they guess—no looking.

WORKING PARENTS/BUSY FAMILIES

While grocery shopping/mall shopping:

Count how many steps it will take you to get to your desired destination.

Give your child a list of things to find (they have to stay with you at all times).

Three items I suggest you never leave home without: a small note pad, pens or pencils, and a book. There are so many activities that you can do at every age with just these few things.

More play activities in back of the book!

Children at Work

Have you ever noticed how easy it is for a child to make play out of anything at any time? Play happens so naturally for young children that it doesn't take much thought or planning. Children between ages zero and five are considered to be working as they play. This is because they are gaining so much information through the process. This stage of development involves sensory learning, which means learning through the use of the mouth, ears, eyes, smell, and touch. If you observe babies, toddlers, and preschoolers, you will notice that just about everything they touch goes in their mouths. Most toys that are geared for young children are made with these concepts in mind. Toys for this age group are textured for touch, colorful for sight, possess sound for hearing, and are chewable for taste. It is truly amazing how much children learn at this stage of development; it is known to be one of the most crucial growth periods.

With all that in mind it is extremely important to foster learning through play. This is one of the easiest times for providing an environment geared for play. Don't feel that you have to go out and buy every toy available. Kids are great inventors—they make up the best games! What we have to be careful of is not putting a child in a room every day and closing the door. Children can benefit from some time to themselves while interacting with materials, but it is just as important to make sure they have the opportunities to interact with other children, too. There needs to be a balance. In either circumstance, they will build skills for independence and self-confidence, as well as engage in interactions that provide rich learning experiences for social growth.

    Children at this stage engage in free play, or play that happens spontaneously. Usually during free play one will choose things of interest, such as painting, reading, building blocks, etc. As we age this becomes more apparent, and many times we even make careers choices from those interests. Examples of free play are when you see your children building a garage of blocks for their cars, or writing "scribbles" on a paper and reading to you, or painting a self portrait. When you find that your child has a particular interest, you can enhance it by making the supplies easily available. But continue to expose them to a variety of things.

Educators, especially early childhood, please hold onto your pretend play corners. If you are like me, you are feeling the pull from the powers to be to phase them out. We know that children learn just as much in these areas as they do with reading, writing, and arithmetic. Parents, support your children's teachers to promote some play in their day. Trust that your child will learn and that play time will not take away from that; it will only enhance it.

This is such a great stage; it sets the tone for many years by promoting positive feelings of play. Encouraging positive feelings also reinforces social/emotional development. This is the area where children learn about their feelings and how to express them. It is imperative that every individual feels comfortable and confident with their emotions. Our feelings are part of our personality. Children need to be praised often and told that they are loved daily. These key concepts will create a sense of security, which builds self-confidence. We all know how the confidence we have or don't have in ourselves is an integral part of all we encounter. Everyone deserves to feel good about themselves. As parents and educators, we need to continually reinforce skills that will promote the building of self-confidence: risk taking, independence, empathy, and problem solving. When children are able to experience dealing with problems and mistakes, we are preparing them to handle anything that's thrown at them, good or bad. Our state of mind has a huge impact on our successes in life. Think positive, live positive!

Activities
General activities/items of interest according to developmental age groups

INFANT

rattles
music
books
chew toys
mirrors
mobiles
rocking equipment
pat-a-cake
peek-a-boo
soft toys
colorful items
soft blankets
squeaky toys
sensory items
spongy balls

C'MON EVERYBODY LET'S PLAY!

TODDLER/PRESCHOOLER

trikes/riding toys
puzzles
bubbles
swings
sand play
building blocks
books
bug exploration
dance
listen to music
play dough
painting
coloring
water play
housekeeping items—play dishes, clothes
play animals
balls
simple games
balance board
jumping on cushions
songs
finger plays
stuffed animals
tearing paper
nursery rhymes
puppets balls
cars/trucks

CHILDREN AT WORK

dolls
shape toys
hide-n-seek
Ring around the Rosie
London Bridge
Duck Duck goose

C'MON EVERYBODY LET'S PLAY!

<u>SCHOOL AGE</u>
art and craft supplies
LEGO toys
obstacle course
collections
hopscotch
jump rope
music
books
makeup
magazines
board games
marbles
balls
paint
bikes
sport equipment
playing cards

Developing Social Skills

It is important to know some of the skills that children need to practice and strengthen for social development. The list includes behaviors that children and adults use on a daily basis. All of these life skills give us the tools to use with each other in our everyday world.

Sharing
Patience
Empathy
Respect
Cooperation
Friendship
Kindness
Responsibility
Independence
Confidence
Problem Solving
Risk Taking

Remember a child cannot be expected to share if they haven't been taught, or they can't be confident if no one has built their self-esteem.

As parents and educators, we continually need to model and reinforce the skills. As you work on these skills through play, remember to encourage language. Ask questions and create conversations; verbal skills are important in expressing ourselves. Children will be in many situations where they will need to speak for themselves, whether positive or negative, but they need to be heard and communicate with confidence.

An example of this might be as you are play-acting a trip to the zoo and you are pretending to be the animals. Ask your children why they chose a specific animal and what they know about that animal. The conversation will take over naturally. You can even bring in some facts and knowledge and use your imaginations to make up a new kind of animal.

When dealing with older children who may be facing a situation with peers, you might also use this method of questioning with them. It will enhance their ability to be confident enough to discuss their feelings and then work out some problem-solving strategies.

Some ways to emphasize these skills during play at any age are as follows:

- Play games with your child. Don't let them always win, and teach them how to be a good sport.

DEVELOPING SOCIAL SKILLS

- Don't have too many toys; then children can learn to take turns and share.
- Be ready to support your child if you see them getting frustrated with something. Show them how to slow down, take their time and be patient.
- Let them be in charge of the activity. It will build independence and responsibility.
- If someone gets hurt during a game or activity, show them how to help others, thus promoting empathy.
- When a child is feeling left out, teach your child how to invite them into their play, developing kindness and friendship.
- Create a situation where you or another child may need help completing a task. Cooperation and teamwork will surely do the trick.

As you are strengthening each skill, always use positive words of encouragement and praise. Let your child know that you are there for them when they need support.

Disciplined Play

I am sure you are wondering how and why play can be disciplined. Playing does not mean a "free for all." Although play can appear to be unstructured craziness at times, it does have structure.

If you watch people playing, you will see there is some kind of plan, purpose, or goal being achieved. It may be as simple as building the biggest tower, winning a game, bonding with family and friends, or playing to have fun. There is also a beginning, middle, and end to the play process. Children learn the unspoken mechanics, and they learn about rules. They learn that if they want to play, they will need to clean up. If they want a playmate, they will need to share, and if they play a game, they have to follow the rules. Through the process, guidelines will be established. This is where the discipline comes in for the adult. We need to make sure the rules are followed as children are first learning them.

Remember children will not know what to do until they have experienced it; the younger they are, the more limited their experience. We need to model the expected behavior (cleaning up, for example), then make sure there is follow through. It's like when I cook a meal. Even though I don't like washing the dishes, I know that it's something that has to be done in order for me to eat. The best way to approach the rules with children is by adding some fun. If your child likes music, play his/her favorite song while cleaning. Try sorting toys by colors as you put them away, and so on. There will be times, too, that rules don't seem very fun, and that's okay. Children learn life lessons this way— even lessons that they may not like but have a purpose (example: your bedtime is eight).

Although we need to let children learn, explore, and practice through play, there will also be times where we need to redirect their behaviors or choices. If you see or hear your child doing something that is not appropriate, you need to step in. Whether it's hitting another child or the use of bad language, you need to act on the misbehavior immediately. As children get older, let them work out their own solutions using the tools you have given them. Disciplining a child means teaching the child what you expect. They truly may not know what they did wrong. Discipline does not mean having to yell,

DISCIPLINED PLAY

harm physically, or shame emotionally. It does mean respecting your child enough to discuss the problem, to say "no" firmly, and to use natural consequences—"You won't play again with your toys until you put them away." When you show respect to your child, the more likely they are to respect you.

There are hundreds of books that parents can find on the topic of disciplining children from birth to teen. There are many different styles and theories, so you will need to find the one that best fits you. Being consistent is one of the most important aspects of discipline, but it is often the hardest. We feel like a broken record at times, but we need to stick with the goal and keep reinforcing the desired behavior. Sometimes we have had enough, or maybe we're just too tired to follow through. You probably know by now that children can sense when they can take advantage of us. They even know our weaknesses!

Children like structure. They need to know the boundaries. These provide a sense of security and the feeling of being loved and cared for. You will definitely need to put the time and energy into helping your child learn to make good choices and decisions, which will benefit them in the years to come.

Outdoor Play and Organized Sports

Do you remember the days of playing tag, kick the can, riding bikes, and coming home when the street lights came on? These are great memories for some of us, and although times are somewhat different now, we know how important and fun it is to be outside playing. Outside play in all kinds of weather has many great benefits, such as building and strengthening all the large muscles, promoting exercise and healthy bodies, stress release, and engaging in a multitude of learning activities—and let's not forget the sheer enjoyment! Typically, playing outdoors involves family, friends, and neighbors, which again is developing one's social skills.

The unfortunate problem that many families face today, unlike in the past, is the fear of letting children play outdoors as freely as we did when we were young. Because we are concerned about the safety of our children, and rightly so, many of them are not getting to enjoy all the wonders and learning that comes with being outside. I had a family a couple of years ago who told me that their five-year-old boy was not allowed to go out to play because they did not feel comfortable or safe in their neighborhood. The only opportunity the child had to be outside with peers was at school.

Imagine all the children who may be in this same predicament. What a travesty, but well understood. Although we clearly have some obstacles to face, such as safety and time constraints, we know the positive impact outdoor play has on our children, so we need to put in the extra effort and be creative. Find parents in your neighborhood with whom you feel comfortable and take turns watching the kids outside. Seek out playmates from school and plan to meet at local parks and playgrounds, parents included. Once you provide the environment, the children will provide the imagination (see activity list in back).

Organized sports are a little bit more of a challenge. Sports provide some great character building skills as well as keeping children occupied in a healthy, fun way—taking turns, teamwork, problem solving, cooperation, empathy, and more. The down side of team sports is often the adults.

A lot of pressure is put on children who are involved in sports physically and mentally.

OUTDOOR PLAY AND ORGANIZED SPORTS

Depending on the situation, sport teams can be rough on kids. Not only do the players have to meet the expectations of their parents and themselves, but also the coaches. There are many fantastic coaches out there. Unfortunately there are some who are not and they can have a negative effect on children.

As children get older, they are faced with trying out for teams and the reality of being cut. Sometimes the process is handled fairly by the adult coaches. Other times we deal with systems that are tainted because of other factors that come into play (human error, favoritism, opinions, etc.). If you read some of the professional athlete books, you will see this firsthand. Their words can encourage children. Children learn these hard life lessons fast. This is where all your hard work from laying a solid foundation in early childhood pays off. Telling your children daily to believe in themselves and that you believe in them and love them will also give them the confidence they need to face any encouragement or discouragement they may encounter.

Having three sons, I have certainly had my share of seeing firsthand all the dynamics in sporting events. I have witnessed parents being thrown out of baseball parks, coaches being fouled for poor behavior, and players left crying and embarrassed. I understand the meaning of "winning," but we all need to remember it *is* supposed to be fun. I have seen the kind coach who makes practice fun and plays games where kids can really learn. And, as parents, we also need to check our behavior. Yelling or criticizing our child from the bleachers is not the solution. We need to provide support and encouragement. Talk with your child privately if you have a concern with their game. Do you think that they want everyone to be aware of their mistake? Do you think they did it on purpose to make you mad? When we make mistakes as adults, are they intentional? Do we want to be reprimanded in front of a crowd? I think not. Always, always put yourself in your child's shoes; see things from their eyes, no matter what age they are.

If you know anyone or have a child yourself involved in a sport, you know that it can consume all of your time as well as your child's. Even though a specific sport is played in a particular season, nowadays you can turn it in to a year-round event, almost like a job. I have seen some teenagers practicing for three sports at one time because they don't want to miss out or they don't want a coach to think they are not trying hard enough. Does this seem as overwhelming to you as it does to me? Sometimes we get caught up in the "more is better" school of thought. Again, it's great to help your children become the best they can and to achieve their goals, but don't do it at the cost of missing out on being a kid and enjoying carefree days. I have heard many coaches say that there's more to being an athlete than playing the game. They like to see sportsmanship, teamwork, risk taking, confidence, respect, and problem solving. Where do we learn these skills? You got it—play, free play. Coaches, as you encourage your kids to work hard, also do them the favor of giving them time to play hard.

The key to sports and outdoor play is getting out there, doing it, and having fun. Children can benefit so much from each other and the many skills involved as well as gaining some lifelong friendships. Some schools are even finding themselves cutting recess from their day because of budget cuts, staffing, and demanding academics. This is an unfortunate problem for our children. As mentioned earlier, recess is the only form of outdoor play some children are getting. The loss of recess would surely affect children's need for exercise, as well as its importance in learning many of life's social/emotional skills they will need in years to come. Throughout our school days, we learned a lot about what's been called the big playground of life.

Teen Play

Teens need play time, too. Remember I said earlier that everyone should be playing and it should be age appropriate? Try to think back when you were a teen, I bet some of your fondest memories came from hanging out with peers. It is actually a form of play. Not only do our teens have an enormous amount of school work to tend to but they usually have a rigid extracurricular calendar. When do they get time for themselves?

Times are very different for teens now than they were for you and me. Cell phones and texting have taken over; how did we ever live without them? Inventions are great, but we always need to understand how they affect us. Teens like texting because they can be in contact with their peers, and isn't that what being a teen is about? We cannot allow it to take over their social interactions with others. If you have a teen, you may have noticed that talking to others, or should I say talking with adults, is not one of their favorite things to do. I have two teenage boys, I can vouch for them.

Please don't let your teens get out of the habit of talking with others; provide social situations where they can respond to and interact in conversations. Communication skills do not only mean talking with others, they also include: facial gestures, eye contact, confidence, and being a good listener, to a name a few. What I mean by this is that teenagers will soon be growing into young adults, and as young adults they need to be good communicators. They will need to speak for themselves in many situations as we will not be there to assist them. Hopefully, we have modeled the social behaviors as well as good communication skills along their childhood journey so they can be independent, verbal, social beings.

When considering play time for your teen, which does not mean the same here as it does for a younger child, you will find that it is a time to connect with peers who typically have the same interests. It may even just be time to hang out, listen to music and talk. Play takes on many new forms as we grow older. It basically means to have some fun however we may interpret it, but in a safe, responsible way.

If at all possible try to encourage your child to play with the family. Try to find the common thread that will keep you and your teen connected. Create some fun ideas/activities that aren't too overwhelming; they are more apt to join in when it seems more natural. Plan some fun dinners that include great conversation. Don't focus on homework or stressful things—lighten up and talk about things that you might have laughed about in the past or reminisce about when they were younger.

Teens are living in a fast-paced world filled with some unpleasant realities that aren't so nice. We can help our teens by providing them with an outlet, such as play, as they face intense academics and increased exposure to drugs, alcohol, divorce, effects of the media, and a struggling economy. These changes in our society are known to cause stress in our children, which is displayed through anger, anxiety, impulsiveness, emotional issues, and pressure that leads to overwhelming low self-esteem.

Educators and parents need to realize the stress that is put on our children in every aspect of their lives. Now more than ever we need to make sure that we are providing them with time for fun, play, and relaxation. Our society has become achievement obsessed, and in the process we have forgotten the well-being of our children.

I think you would agree with me that it's definitely worth the effort to include some play in your teen's day. It will help your children have a happier, more balanced life.

C'MON EVERYBODY LET'S PLAY!

There are activities in the back of the book to help get you started. Once you get the hang of it, you will be able to create suitable activities that fit your family's lifestyle and interests.

TEENS
board games
music
books
skateboarding
jewelry
knitting
sewing
hobbies
collections
lawn games—badminton, croquet, horseshoes, etc.
Sports—basketball, hockey, tennis, baseball, lacrosse, swimming, volleyball, softball, etc.
weight lifting
dance
ice/roller skating
shopping

Homework vs. Play

I am sure you can imagine how I feel about the title of this chapter! Have you asked your child or other parents lately how they feel about homework, and, just as importantly, how they feel about the amount of homework their child is given each night? Do they find that it causes stress in their home and that is has even taken over weekends and holidays?

Does homework affect other members of your family in that they do not get the attention that they need? I have talked to many parents and found that they are so stressed by the amount of homework given that many of the parents themselves are completing it so their children can get to bed at a decent time and be ready for school the next day. Although homework definitely has its place in our children's lives, it should not take over the majority of their life.

Far too often I see homework assignments given as just more work for a student to do, with no real connection to how the material can be used and applied in the world around them. Usually work that is given as homework is what we refer to as "busy" work, or time fillers.

Some teachers feel that if they give homework, they are better teachers. Sometimes we feel that parents want it for their children, so we might as well appease them. Homework might also be work that did not get completed throughout the day. This is not the fault of the teacher, but the effect of an overwhelming amount of curriculum and statewide tests. Many times teachers are being given more curricula than can be accomplished, or a student doesn't complete the work for lack of understanding or other various reasons.

If you feel that your child is getting the right amount of homework, that's great. Homework can benefit students by getting them in the habit of doing it, as well as teaching organizational skills and time management. Children learn about the work ethic—that if they work hard they will achieve their goals. As a teacher, I set high expectations for my students, as well as for my own children. I expect students to perform to the best of their ability. Keep in mind though this doesn't mean overdoing, pushing, or causing stress to a student. We know that these tactics will only become a detriment to their learning. If you ever have any concerns regarding the amount of work or the purpose of the work, it

HOMEWORK VS. PLAY

is important for you and your child to discuss it as well as contact the teacher.

When parents of kindergarteners ask me for homework, I let them know there are many great workbooks available at the local stores, but that reading and creating meaningful learning experiences at home are the best kind of work for children. Meaningful learning experiences are representations of what has been learned and put into action so that it is being applied in our everyday lives.

Examples of this according to age group would be:

> Preschool: When children are learning colors at school, they can play a game at home in which they look for things of specific colors. "Find me something red," or "Find me something blue and round." These activities can then be carried out wherever they go, at Grandma's, the grocery store, or while waiting in the doctor's office.
>
> School Age: After a unit on butterflies, house some caterpillars and let your child tell you about the lifecycle. Have your child make a book about butterflies and paint the pictures accordingly after finding some in your yard.

Middle School: As the students learn about their heritage and ancestry, spend time with a grandparent to share their wealth of knowledge. It not only provides learning family history, but bonding among generations.

High School: When out shopping, ask your children to calculate the tax for you. Another idea is when your family is at a restaurant let them add in the amount of tip. Give your child a specific amount of money and give them a list of items to be bought at the grocery store.

Of course there are many, many more ideas that you can create to provide those meaningful learning experiences. Once you start, it gets easier. What is so wonderful about this is that instead of filling out worksheets or doing paper/pencil tasks, our children are actually using and applying what they have learned. When we actually experience something, we are more apt to understand it and make use of it.

The more real-life experiences that you can provide for your children, the better equipped and well rounded they become for what lies ahead.

Try these: trips to farmers' market, museums, foot trails, nature centers, aquariums, farm, zoo, or apple orchard.

We know realistically that children will have homework in their day. Teach your child how to make homework fun; it makes learning easy. Help your child manage their schedule to include time for play. Whether they choose to play first (as many children need to do) or do homework first, or even alternate the two, make play a priority. A little fun will go a long way; it will rejuvenate our children for school and the other activities in their lives.

Technology and Media

Wow, who would have ever thought we'd be where we are today with technology? Sometimes I can't even wrap my mind around how it all works, and I always feel at least one step behind. This is the world in which our children live. It's commonplace for them, and they are good at it.

I am constantly amazed at how easy it is to find any information on the World Wide Web that one desires. It can be so helpful and provide instant knowledge. As parents, we need to be responsible for how our children are using this medium. There are a multitude of games and websites available at the click of one's mouse. I am sure I don't have to tell you the plethora of sites that prey on our children. Again, like with all other things, there is the good and the bad. We just need to pursue the best for our children. Playing games on the computer as well as using video games can be fun and can also provide some beneficial learning if appropriate. It is important for us to monitor the time and usage our children spend with technology. I worry that children are spending more time playing computer games than playing outdoor games, missing the opportunities to engage in those meaningful learning experiences.

Media, television, newspaper, and radio can also have somewhat of the same effect on children. Too much of these can result in the loss of social interactions and time to explore their world. The media also plays a strong role in many of our children's choices, attitudes, and behaviors. Much of the programming that we are exposed to will try to persuade us in some way: buy something that's new and improved, be someone better. It sets our children up for misconceptions and unrealistic expectations. What also worries me is the amount of adult information to which children are continually being exposed. It is hard to turn the news on, either radio or TV, without hearing about unpleasant events.

It is one thing to teach our children about what may be happening in our world, but it needs to be done age appropriately and they do not need to know everything. I have had many children come to school worried about news events that they may have heard that particular morning. The children become stressed because they do not always understand what they heard and often become frightened that whatever it was will happen to them. Remember some of the news they hear is out of their realm of comprehension. The reality of it can even be hard for us to swallow. If you feel strongly about informing your child about something that you feel is relevant to them, absolutely take the time to discuss it with them. We do need to help them be aware of their safety, their living environment, and anything that affects their immediate world. If you find that your child is overwhelmed about something they have heard, talk about it with them. You can also act it out through play. Remember how play can help a child understand events and make them meaningful.

Keep in mind also that the commercials our children see and hear have a big impact on them. Sometimes they learn a product's jingle before the ABC song! Ads can be stereotypical toward males and females and create false expectations. We see that most women on television are thin, shapely, and beautiful. Men are strong and drink beer. When children see this enough, they think it's the norm and that it will make them happy, too. Propaganda can be very enticing.

As with technology, media can also provide quality learning and enjoyment. There are many great TV shows that are geared toward children, teens, and adults. We can teach our children to make good choices in what they watch and the amount of time of they watch.

Think about it this way. Watching and doing are two different actions—which one would you choose?

Play in the Adult World

As an adult you are probably not even consciously aware of when you are playing. If you stop to think about it, it's the times you find yourself laughing or having a good time with peers, coworkers, or family. It's that "feel good" moment you've experienced and will remember the most at the end of the day.

Play has a different purpose for adults than for children. We can still learn through play, but most often the benefits we reap come in the forms of stress relief, health, enjoyment, and social interactions. As we age, our friends become even more important to us. Not only do they become companions, but they become our support systems. We share our ideas and thoughts with them. Often they become our confidants.

Many places of employment provide team-building events in order to get the staff excited and motivated about working together. These activities help form relationships so coworkers can learn about each other, creating a positive work environment. It also aids in developing effective communication, problem-solving techniques, and a sense of camaraderie.

To some of us having a little fun in our work environment seems normal, but for others it may be a little more difficult. Of course the type of job you are in has something to do with it; some workplaces, and bosses, are just more conducive for playing than others. A prime example of having fun while working is on the TV show *Ace of Cakes*. Duff Goldman and his staff make the most amazing cake creations while having a great time. Part of the secret to their good fortune is their enjoyment of working together. The program shows us that pairing fun and hard work makes a great recipe for success. If possible take the first step in adding some play to your work day. Start simple with a funny comment. Hopefully, others will join in; it can surely be infectious. You will find your workday seems more enjoyable and the time goes more quickly when you have fun.

Incorporating fun into your daily life, outside of work, can be just as easy because you have the control. Taking time for yourself does not mean you are being selfish, it means you care enough about your well-being. You can include your family in your play, or find separate time for both. Being positive and confident are probably the two most important characteristics for incorporating play. Start with an interest, and the enjoyment is certain to come.

Play can be whatever you want it to be for you. Join a league, class, or club. There are lots of them (bowling, golf, scrapbooking, service clubs, etc.). If you have a hobby, find others with the same interests and plan time to get together. You will soon find your friendships will flourish. Just getting together to share and compare life stories can bring an evening of enjoyment.

It is just as important to take time to play for yourself as it is for your children. Look at our senior citizens. They are great role models; they always seem to be having so much fun. Most likely they have become good at it because they have had the most experience with it. They know the benefits and rewards it provides. Take time to unite children and grandparents. Grandparents have so much to offer our children. As George Bernard Shaw says, with great wisdom, "We don't stop playing because we grow old; we grow old because we stop playing."

C'MON EVERYBODY LET'S PLAY!

ADULTS
playing cards
board games
exercise classes
music
dance
golf
bird watching
bingo
shopping
collections
hobbies
gardening
cooking
bowling
horseshoes

Including All Children

There are many children born into this world who have a disability of some type.

Some are obvious to the human eye, while others are not. You probably know someone who has a child with a special need, or you may be experiencing it yourself.

Please know that children with disabilities like to play, too. We need to make sure that we include them in our play times. Not only will we help all children learn to be empathetic toward each other, but we are also teaching them the importance of uniqueness and that we can learn so much from each other's strengths. When we encourage children to play with others and become aware of the differences, we are teaching them important life skills that they will use in years to come.

Children are usually the most accepting of differences in others and will become accepting teenagers and so on if we model and foster positive behaviors and attitudes. Hopefully, by uniting all children through a universal activity such as play, this generation will celebrate each other for who they are.

Some special needs that you may encounter in individuals include:

> Physical disability (child may be in a wheel chair)
> Autism (child may lack social and communication skills)
> Hearing or vision (loss of)
> ADHD (types of attention deficit disorder)
> Anxiety disorders

These are just a few; there are many more disabilities with which children are dealing.

It is important for you to communicate with a child's parent so you can be educated and feel comfortable. Don't worry about your child; they usually know more than we do. They have had the opportunity to become familiar with all types children. Many of these children are being mainstreamed into classrooms so they can be with their peers and in the best possible learning environment. Who better to learn from? It is definitely a win-win situation!

The key to peer play is to find a common interest, something that the children like to do together, just as adults tend to seek out others who like

INCLUDING ALL CHILDREN

the same things. Because of the different learning styles some of these children possess, their play may look a little nontraditional. Relax; the children know what to do instinctively. If you ever have questions, be sure to ask the families with whom you are sharing play; they will be happy to provide awareness and answers.

Examples of interests:
    Sports—baseball, football, etc.
    Games—checkers, chess
    Collections—baseball cards, coins,
    Shopping—clothes, interest
    Hobby—knitting, painting

Play is not picky about who engages in it or how someone looks. It doesn't want to judge us, it just wants to be enjoyed by all.

Conclusion

My goal in writing this book and sharing this information is to give you the tools, knowledge, and encouragement to use the power of play to your advantage.

We know we are facing tough times, families are struggling, educators are being challenged, and children are losing their childhood. Upon implementing some of the strategies provided, you can make a difference each and every day by giving your children and yourself time and permission to play. Still, after all the years that I have taught kindergarten the most frequently asked question as children enter the classroom is "When are we going to play?". Remember the key is to balance play and work. I am confident that you and your family will experience a change for the better, which will result in strengthening your family bond. My desire is that everyone will find the fun and happiness they so richly deserve.

I am hoping that you have sensed my passion throughout the book. I know that together we can give our children this special gift—the gift of play.

C'MON EVERYBODY LET'S PLAY!

Remember it doesn't have to cost you anything, just your heart and soul.

In closing I believe that Peggy Ann McKay says it best in this Shel Silverstein poem:

"I cannot go to school today," said little Peggy Ann McKay.
"I have the measles and the mumps, a gash, a rash, and purple bumps. My mouth is wet, my throat is dry, I'm going blind in my right eye...
What's that?
What's that you say?
You say today is...
Saturday?
G'bye, I'm going out to play!"
Shel Silverstein
(1932–1999)

Activities for Play

These are activities that I have done with either my own children or my kindergarten children, so they are tried and true! I have chosen not to put the activities into age categories. You will find that many of these will overlap in the stages of development as in the previous pages. Since every individual develops according to their own needs, you can use them when desired. Most of the activities can be enjoyed at any age. Just adjust them accordingly to what the child can do.

For more ideas use your resources, share ideas with other parents, and use the Internet. I get a lot of ideas when I go to my local dollar store. There are many great items for a small price that can be turned into hours of fun when combined with some imagination.

Please feel free to contact me for any questions you may have regarding the activities.

C'MON EVERYBODY LET'S PLAY!

So come on *everybody* let's play!!

INDOOR ACTIVITIES

- ❖ String pasta noodles or fruit ring cereal on a piece of yarn to make a necklace or bracelet.
- ❖ Make colors by mixing food colors together in baby jars so you can see the changes.
- ❖ Bring snow in the house and put in the kitchen sink. Give your child scoops and cups to play with.
- ❖ Make snow ice cream: add milk and sugar.
- ❖ Bake together. If you have a teen, let them choose and prepare the meal with your assistance.
- ❖ Play music and dance. Create dance routines.
- ❖ Hand clapping games. Clap hands to make rhythms or look up clapping games such as Miss Mary Mack or A Sailor Went to Sea.
- ❖ Make a family band. Use homemade instruments.
- ❖ Make a fort. Use bed sheets and attach to chairs or hang over tables.
- ❖ Have an indoor picnic.

ACTIVITIES FOR PLAY

- ❖ Make a treasure hunt. Hide an item and make written clues for everyone to follow.
- ❖ Act out stories like *Three Little Pigs*. Take turns playing different characters. You can make puppets for this by using socks.
- ❖ Play the bus game. Line up chairs in a bus formation. Sing "Wheels on The Bus" as you pretend being passengers.
- ❖ Point to a spot on the globe with your eyes closed. Find out information about the location; imagine what it would be like to live there.
- ❖ Get some large boxes to color and cut to make as props. Make a spaceship while being an astronaut, a cave for a bear, etc.
- ❖ Lay large sheets of paper on your kitchen table; let the kids decorate using markers for your dinner tablecloth.
- ❖ Play charades.
- ❖ Have a tea party.
- ❖ Fill a bag with odds and ends. Each child puts hand in and makes a guess by the feel of each item.
- ❖ Make shapes, letters, and design with shaving cream, pudding paint, or finger paint.

C'MON EVERYBODY LET'S PLAY!

- ❖ Have a craft tub available with items for children to create with: paper, paper towel rolls, pipe cleaners, tissue paper, scissors, glue, ribbon, stickers, etc.
- ❖ Make your own crayons with broken bits and pieces from old crayons. Take the papers off and place pieces in muffin tins or baking molds and bake in oven.
- ❖ Give your children each a spring-loaded clothespin. Throw clean socks from the laundry basket on the floor; have them find matches, attach with a clothespin, and place back in laundry basket.
- ❖ Fill a balloon with air. Each player has to tap it gently to keep it in the air. Variations to the game include: sit on floor, kneel down, use only your finger to tap the balloon—just don' let it touch the ground!
- ❖ Play hot potato using a real potato (not cooked); pretend it is hot and pass it fast. Color a face on it with a permanent marker.
- ❖ Play Three Clues. Each day one family member gives three clues to where they have hidden a specified item. The person who finds the item gets to be the hider next time.

ACTIVITIES FOR PLAY

- Use store-bought letter pretzels to write your name and to spell other words.
- Use store-bought animal crackers to play many games. Grab an animal, make that animals sound while the other players guess. Find matches for the animals and sort them.
- Using paper and markers, take turns drawing the capital letters of the alphabet. Turn them into a picture.
- Play hangman with paper and pencil.
- Play tic-tac-toe with paper and pencil.
- Two fun games great for the car: Skip a Number and Skip a Letter. Skip a Number goes like this: Before you begin choose a number that has to be omitted while counting, such as five. Everyone begins to count but has to skip any number with a five in it. Continue until someone misses. This game can be adjusted to make harder for older children by using addition or multiplication. In Skip a Letter, use your imagination to determine the rules, such as skip any letter that has a slanted line (A, K, M, N, R, V, W, X, Y, Z), then begin saying the alphabet skipping those letters. Change the directions each time (can't make the

- "s" sound, etc.). These games really work the brain!
- Another great game for the car is the rhyming game. The first player says any word, then each player has to rhyme that word. It can be a real word or made-up word. The game continues until a player has run out of words, then that player can start a new round with a new word.
- Concentration is another game for the car, or anywhere. Play this game by choosing a category, such as pets, girl names, sports, and then each player contributes an answer until someone is stumped.
- Set up pretend play stations using props. One day make a pizza shop, a doctor's office, or a veterinary using stuffed animals. Add items to each station by searching around the house, or make your own with paper and crayons.
- Magazines can provide lots of fun for play and learning. Children can cut out favorite pictures to make a collage for a room. Find letters in names and make a name plate, add decorations.
- Give each person in the family paper, pencils, and markers. Everyone is to create their dream house adding everything

ACTIVITIES FOR PLAY

they would want in their house. Encourage them to use their imaginations, and then everyone shares their ideas with the family.
- ❖ Make bird feeders with empty milk cartons.
- ❖ At dinner, each person takes a turn sharing: the best part of their day, a plan for weekend fun, something funny that happened. Pick one only for each meal; this helps develop communication.
- ❖ Use a cookie sheet and sprinkle some salt or sugar to fill the bottom. Children can write or draw in it using their fingertips.
- ❖ Do some simple science experiments. Baking soda, pop, and other household items can be great ingredients.
- ❖ Family movie night- each family member takes a turn choosing the movies.
- ❖ Camping indoors.
- ❖ Family game night.
- ❖ Make decorations for holidays and hang them in your house.

OUTDOOR ACTIVITIES

- "Paint" the house using a bucket of water and different size paintbrushes.
- Fill spray bottles with water and squirt each other. Can add food coloring to water, but remind children only to spray driveways and sideways!
- Use large sponges to soak up water from a bucket. Throw or squish the sponges on the cement and make designs.
- Bury trinkets in the sand box and invite children to go on a treasure hunt. I like to bury tooth picks and tell children to pretend to be a paleontologist and dig for dinosaur bones. It's fun to dig with tongs, tweezers, and berry hullers.
- Play in the snow; make snow angels, snow people, snow paths for running.
- Splash in the rain puddles.
- Walk in the rain with no umbrella (not in storms).
- Play flashlight tag at night.
- Chase butterflies.
- Camp in the backyard, make s'mores.
- Have fun with bubbles, make your own. There are many bubble recipes. Try liquid dish soap and sugar. Cut out your own

ACTIVITIES FOR PLAY

bubble blowers from margarine lids and other containers.
- Make an obstacle course. Use items you find in your garage.
- Plant a garden.
- Catch fireflies in a jar.
- Have a picnic.
- Jump rope; learn some jump rope chants for added fun.
- Run through the sprinkler.
- Lawn games: hot box, bean bag game, Frisbee, croquet, etc.
- Sidewalk chalk.
- Riding bikes, scooters.
- Sport games.
- Mother, May I?
- Simon Says.
- Red Light, Green Light.
- What Time Is It, Mr. Fox?
- Have a mini-triathlon by using three favorite sports.
- Play waffle ball.
- Jacks.
- Capture the flag.
- Kick ball.
- Riding bikes.
- Flying kites.
- Scavenger hunt.

C'MON EVERYBODY LET'S PLAY!

Here are some suggestions for great meaningful learning experiences. These are trips that you and your family can enjoy for free or at a minimal cost, depending on where you live.

picnics
going to the beach
the zoo
fish hatchery
aquarium
butterfly garden
park
nature preserve
museum
plays at local theater
farmers market
playgrounds
fruit farms
outdoor concerts
animal farms
train station
star gazing